MW00490006

Poems

Poems

Grace Zabriskie

The New York Quarterly Foundation, Inc.
New York, New York

NYQ Books™ is an imprint of The New York Quarterly Foundation, Inc.

The New York Quarterly Foundation, Inc.
P. O. Box 2015
Old Chelsea Station
New York, NY 10113

www.nyqbooks.org

Copyright © 2010 by Grace Zabriskie

All rights reserved. No part of this book may be used or reproduced in any manner whatsoever without written permission of the author. This book is a work of fiction. Any references to historical events, real people or real locales are used fictitiously. Other names, characters, places, and incidents are products of the author's imagination, and any resemblance to actual events or locales or persons, living or dead, is entirely coincidental.

I would like to acknowledge Faith Sale, editor of *New Writing; The Book-of-the-Month Club College English Association Award Anthology*, and Raymond Hammond, editor of *The New York Quarterly,* for previously publishing poems contained within these pages.

First Edition

Set in Myriad Pro

Layout and Design by Raymond P. Hammond
Cover Art: "Chasing the Rabbit," 17" x 24", acrylic on panel; by Marion Lane—www.marionlane.com

Library of Congress Control Number: 2009933867

ISBN: 978-1-935520-05-4

for Helen

Contents

THE CASTLE BUILDS HERSELF

PALE ATLANTA DEALER / THE LEAVER

PHOTOGRAPHABLE VULNERABILITY

Poems

Poems

The Castle Builds Herself

PRINTS IN THE DUST

place in the bedroom floor
where boards creak
gap between them and wall's growing
no one ever steps there
but me
to put prints in the dust

THE CASTLE BUILDS HERSELF

First there is only space,
self contained,
disciplined to know
itself from mere air
and where the boundary lies—
a round one,
pulled up from the ground
like that child's toy,
the slinky rings
that seem content
ascending and descending stairs,
curbs, chairs, and
savoring choices;
like which small, extended hand
next to arch
slowly into.

Like that, but merely air,
round and rising to cleave itself.
Phantasm, really,
projected for protection
from still air
by that which swirls inside it;
the rising column of essence
of castle.

Then comes plaster,
seen by the Essence as carapace
for castle space promising most
in terms of ghosts summoned and banished
through the radiant heat
of plaster setting up,
leaving homeless
pastel holograms, wavering, almost
like the walls themselves
until they rally, hearing,
"These shall be my frescos,"

stiffen, suck the images,
shimmering, in,
to await the
hardening cold.

And so the castle lives awhile,
with her old ghosts, flattened.
Distorted, the frozen swarm
reminds her
of what was once but isn't now.
She knows but can't remember how
she loved, or why…Hush!
She is having
a fresh thought.
She sees what the plaster walls
have wrought; muted, soon
almost colorless dreams
that seem always to have been there.
A part—no, the heart—
of the Essence. They are…
her art!
She has made them. She is a maker of art!

And now the outer walls must rise, stony,
protecting the wellspring inside.
Essence was wellspring, she sees now,
for her silent host,
the ghosts of the frescos;
and her wellspring she knows she must hide.
Stone upon stone the outer walls rise,
and the castle grows,
and sparrows die,
and rabbits are born in their burrows.
As greetings she sends
not her voice
through air
but new plaster wall she has made
and broken
to suck up new ghosts she has flattened.
The robins move to a lower limb
which bears more easily their artful shard,
conceived in memory of him
who died last spring in ovum.

His absence from the nest unnoticed,
joyfully received by ants and roots,
mourned by the sensitive Essence.
The robins are grateful; then they are eaten.
Their ghosts decorate a small shrine
between their tree and the castle.

The castle ages, her frescos fade.
Outside she grows horny and thick.
She tries sending more ghosts
through her halls, but they stop
at the walls and will not stick,
for the heat is gone.
So they stay.
They keep the place, make space
for stacks of shards,
help sell them to those who come to the gate,
but mainly they wait,
hoping to be chosen for shards.

One day a dragon comes to buy.
He too is thick and horny—and big.
The castle keeps him out in the yard,
the ghosts shuffle in and out with shards,
and he eats a bold pig as he views them.
"I like your shards," he says,
"They amuse me.
When I've eaten my fill, I will come inside,
confuse, protect, and abuse you.
Get rid of these ghosts;
I have brought you my own.
I'm too great for your gate.
Take the wall down."

"But how can I trust your ghosts,"
she says, "and the still air
I fear will come with you?
My wellspring deepens with every year;
I must guard it,
though I'm not sure what from."

"We will swirl as one and tolerate that
till the end of the world," he answers.

"As for guarding a spring,
there are too many ways,
and some you don't need at all.
I will fill your great hall,
give you seven small monsters
to wander your dungeons and days."

And it comes to pass
that the seventh monster is born.
But the eighth child swirls
and is air.
She stands in the yard
and learns to contain
and finds the game of the springy toy
and cleaves together with rain and dust,
and sweet monster boys must stand away,
but they don't, and
their ghosts are sucked into plaster.
The castle and her dragon laugh.
The castle loves her dragon.
Together they raise the children up,
and now they are a tower,
tall and slim above strong, blank walls,
winking with seven windows.
The wellspring widens and deepens,
springs a leak,
tunnels out to the moat round the castle.
The dragon swims.
A drawbridge is built, sags, is repaired.
Turrets appear, occasional flags,
new wings for shards and for ghosts.
Yards and gardens and pillars and posts.
The castle is building herself.

CHEAP CHOPSTICKS

I am cheap chopsticks
bound together fragile
by my woeful wooden
crotchbrain
slivery membrane
silvery
slow train
to China.
So bound, thus severed,
still would I take
one great breaking step
for mankind, or a kind moon,
or a man somewhat bright
if only from far away.
But only Chinamen may know me well.
I make love like chopsticks
and break like a (Chinese) woman.

PUBLIC AUCTION

There's a Chinese rug I owned in New Orleans
somewhere out in the world.
and a faded brocade box of clay beads and jade
that smelled of old dust
and amber.
The ball of glass fury, of white ice and flurry,
that I later learned meant not the end of the world
but a year, every year.

They're gone. They were sold at the auction.

There's my father's café, lost in New Orleans,
with his mind
and his heart
too early for his sons to kill him in the normal
way of things.
And his crescent of a bar
designed by the river
of patrons for gin, vermouth, and bourbon.

But they're gone. Bought and sold at the auction.

ON MYSTICISM

Someone goes to enormous trouble
trudging about in the Michigan woods
lugging a gigantic slab

clay? concrete? plaster?

a reversible footprint
Dr. Scholls for the gods
dropping it in the mud at
appropriate intervals
just so that later
at dawn
pleasure
will come
to Bigfoot hunters.

flushing? paleness? sensations of awe?

TWO OLD QUESTIONS

If mysticism is the egg
and religion
the chicken
then
clearly the egg
came first

long before religion
began crossing the road

to leave the egg behind.

ANNOTATED ENTRY
or SWEET ENNUI

ENTRY, September 15, 1976:

I must write it down: I was bored today.
For several minutes, I was bored.
I noticed it, of course, became excited,
lost it,
tried to rest, retrace the way that it had come,
and that seduced, of course, so it was done—
gone.
But I was bored today.
Blessed.

NOTES:

Nine years old, squatting hot in backyard weeds, smelling sex in
broken stalks of tall and prickly weeds, seeing
in that white and sticky smell, a boy child's small white penis,
shown to me,
among the weeds.
Not boring, that sweat, pulp, and milky sex-white heated smell of
small boy's pale new penis. Not boring, but from a time of other
weedy hours lived alone—exquisitely boring—and
this is it
you see
a time before time was born.

My bones knew little then, but they did know that all I knew would
stay and never change, and
no
angel rose behind the pomegranate
in that humid garden of first shivering touches to say that I would leave,
self-banished from that place.

No, if he was there, he lay low, no
blow of trumpet to show me out,
row of swords to bar me back; no,
if he was there,
he lay low.
Later, sex, expected, would have been natural, so there were no
further lyings in the leaves, tryings of now perfect possibilities.
We sat in the street, the boys and I, safe on stoops.

We made fun of everyone to music, those
summers of every night on a stoop—
stone stairs, cool; or pine, and warm, and softer.
Laughter. "Hey, Moose!"
Not boring, those glowing radio tube and cooling pavement scented
nights of tires and feet sounding on the street. New taps, almost
every other week.
Weeds?
Who remembered weeds?
A new smell held the heart, gripped the groin and rose the parental
gorge; grease!
Hair grease. Intrinsically romantic.
Not boring, but from a time of many stoop-spent hours, waiting,
and—this is it, you see—a time before anyone—or anything—
had died and been remembered.

My bones knew more, but little more, and
hadn't the old woman across the street rocked there before I was born?
No more angel and the garden long gone, but didn't she know?
Couldn't she tell?
She could have warned, but she sat still, and rocked, and watched me
with the boys.

The witch!

She knew I knew I would never die.
But she sat still
and rocked
and lied.
And then I left, or someone died.
Boredom slowly gained its insidious appeal;
lonely anodyne for the villain zeal with which I walk this
crooked line toward
myriad uninteresting impossibilities.

Stupid old woman!
Did she blacken the mole, let the nose hairs grow,
did she mumble aloud, allow ends of herbs to show,
wisping from the dark of her bosom so that no child
dared shout witch?
Do I make myself a clown, shout out discovery of me
tumbled into each new psychic ditch,
call out each dead heart end stumbled onto—
so that no one
hoping to be found original
dare call me ridiculous?

Angel, you knew in the garden.
Witch, you could have hissed across the street
that with knowledge of death,
boredom would die,
for all practical purposes,
such as rest.

Peace?
Don't hand me peace!
Might as well hand me weeds, as peace.
Peace exhilarates.
Peace lives, and all that lives walks toward death;
and the mind has its pace, the spirit its will
to waken in dreaming and continue the race toward
stillness,
the end; no
rest for the spirit in sleep.

Where are my small, acceptable deaths?
When the clock ticks without sound, the house has no smell,
the walls have no cracks into heaven or
hell, and no taste can begin
to remember?

Years, rich in sweet ennui, and the roads to them
rotted away.
Gardens and streets full of ghosts in repose,
unknowing,
and no way to go back—
or to stay.

PAST CURRENCIES

Miss Honoree had one breast
less than most folk would
expect from a hostess…
still,
she had one.

Just after our father died,
my sister and I stayed at her house
off St. Charles Avenue in New Orleans,
and there were strawberries
and cream in her refrigerator.

Miss Honoree had no children,
that extra breast,
a dachshund, and a husband
who owned *Roland's Salon de Beauté*.
He gave her platinum hair.

She gave him help, there, in his salon,
striped polo shirts to wear with his
moustache, on his boat,
and ran her house with strawberries
and cream in her refrigerator.

At night we cried.
My sister believed her father had loved
her less—had loved me more. I believed
only that he was God—that he was gone.
We did not console one another much.

Miss Honoree cried, the third morning we
were there. She was tired, from screaming.
We had taken—and divided—and eaten—
all Mr. Roland's strawberries
and cream in her refrigerator.

COME AND TELL ME OF YOUR TRAVELS

I.
They told you,
there,
that some old man could
walk on water.
And you laughed,
and then you saw him do it.

You smile,
here,
whisper
"In Mexico…they got stuff they sorta suck
out of the earth for you, just for visual effects."

I say
now,
laughing,
"Yes.
Welcome home. I too am
beyond benefit of miracles.

II.
You arrived in Lugano
on the day they were reburying Hesse.
A lake is there, you say,
with mountains around
and palm trees are found—in Switzerland!
Imagine!

But what I want to know is
why
Were they reburying Hesse?
Were his bones impeding progress?
Was this an annual event?

When
incidentally
had they dug him up?
Earlier that day?
The week before?

Then,
where
had he been before?
Miles away?
or no farther than the space and time of
echoes blown into coconut conchs
found rotting
on the ground
then seeping out
and down
again?

Why don't you know the answers to these
questions?

III.
Did you really sweat
in the desert?
The only evidence
was salt.

You smile and say flowers
in the desert can be
smelled from miles away.
Fantasy,
to smell an unseen rose.
The scent must be so strong,
you say,
and praise the rose for knowing
the necessity for strength
in a desert
where bees are few
and far between.

If a tree falls
in the forest
Will you hear it?
Even if you're there?

WATCH...

Watch...
when she stretches
as cats do
beside you.
Does she wake?
Or slowly break to some
prehistoric dream of the rack
from back when men found
love unmet worthy of such
symbols as could satisfy
the ache?
Ah...she
takes
the rack,
rather than deny a memory molecule.
(There was never perfect love, but,
somehow,
always the recollection of it.)

AFRAID, LIKE EVE

Here is what I have learned from you;
that I must come to you under covers,
behind branches, afraid, like Eve,
in my hair.

That I and my ruse must be perfect;
no leaf leave a gap, the sheet show no
hollow, my hair warp no space
of despair.

I tell you these sheets will wind me;
these branches erase my place
in the earth, and no one will find me.
No hair, no breasts, no face.

February 12, 1991

Afraid of feeling no fear
and therefore fearing my hope
and all that other predictable jazz,

I said no; that we should wait.
And you said wait
until when.
And I said wait
until it's inevitable.

And we both kind of liked it—
that I said that—
if only because saying it made
inevitability
just a tad more
inevitable.

Later, when the inevitable
had become manifest

and I was unable to stop smiling

and we lay together
overwhelmed by what had happened
by what was happening
overwhelmed by what we knew by then had
always been the huge
inevitability of it all
and I was unable to stop smiling,

and when it was almost inevitable
that I would dream later that night of
floating with you above some vast twinkling
vista,

both of us knowing that no souls
out there could possibly be happier than
we/were
then I kissed you more and knew that
someday
love
would have to be said
out/loud

that the proud swell of your lower lip
would be mine from a certain angle

that a way would be found-
would simply have to be finally found
to make love/stay

and I turned away from fear and hope
and all that other predictable jazz
and bowed
to the inevitable.

OLD WOMAN

I want you to come in here
my dear
explain yourself

tell me about your life
how it is different from mine

what I would never quite
understand
because
times are different now
let us talk about texting
twittering
not thinking about
dying
and that old stand-by, the e-mail
about how it is
and why is it
that your having been born into acceptance
of the transitory nature of love
the irrelevance of preference
the non-existence of meaning
saves you in the end from the pain of
none of it

TIME FOR BED

Again it's time for bed,
so I get into it;
feel sleep…possible.

But bed is only a reproach
and welcomes me not at all.
My small weariness flies away, hides among the too
familiar wrinkles in these sheets. I am tired
of this bed
and feel no grateful ache to stretch upon; I've gone
not nearly far enough since I was
here last, can almost feel the
bedsores
the back cramp
the dead legs
testifying
that nothing has happened today
to separate dark from the dark.

IT'S TRUE

It's true.
I'm not sentimental about animals
or birds
not even when they don't speak English.
The essential otherness
of cats
is a restless-making thing
for me.
Put me
in a room with no
eagles
or pygmies
or dolphins
or lions
or Martians
or robins
or apes
or other
time-skippers, culture-jumped mind-grippers
and expect me to sit back and relax, read, do
whatever it is I do.

Problem enough
for me
to trust people from Maine
or other clean, blue, spruce-tree people
when I
in warmth
and brown rot
was born under a banana tree.

Problem enough
for me
to feel reasonably sure

of the relevance of any other Americans of my own
age, sex, and general experience—
sure enough, that is—
to read, sleep, eat, work
thoughtlessly
even when I might be
watching
still hoping
to understand.
For a chance to learn to speak with
dolphins
whales
I would give up
my house
with its beautiful, crumbling walls.

I will go to Venus in a minute
when this is possible
if there are beings there
if perhaps they will not kill me
and if, when my mind becomes exhausted
overloaded,
I can come back.

But don't ask me to live
with a cat.
Spend every day
stupid
other
tempted
even
finally
perhaps
in desperation
to console myself with the similarities of organism.
He eats. I eat.
He shits. I shit.
etcetera
etcetera

until I dull myself sufficiently
to eat
(with good digestion)
while he watches me
from his chair,
to imagine
(if I think of him at all)
that he waits for scraps
or is enjoying the fire
dull myself
sufficiently
(if I think of him at all)
not to wonder
how
he waits
without words
or awareness
of who
is waiting
or warming himself.
Relentless reminder of unspeakable loss
yes
that's part of it.

Easier to conceive God than
waiting
without
"I'm waiting"
easier to remember womb
than bliss
before the word
woe
even wonder
before the words.
Birds.
Hungry, thirsty, urgent throbs
hardly more than pulse and bone
some feathers and a fierceness
to feed

mate
warn
fly
they/ barely make it, you know?
They do die for lack of so little.
Are they sweet?
Is Medea adorable?

Animals in cages are abominations.
We are all of us
therefore
to some degree
abominations, aware
afraid
knowing
that one abomination freeing
another
or itself
risks always smaller cages.

Still
it's true
making love at dusk
I have heard them
birds
outside my window.

I have raised up
looked out
through loose-woven curtains
and window bars
hoping
to complete an impression.

DON'T LOOK FOR REASONS

don't look for reasons to be happy there are none
there is only choosing to be happy anyway
and you can do it
the strength of desperation'll get you there
'f you're open to it

BAD HOSTESS

I care only what is said
before
during
and after
a dinner party.
Not what is presented to be eaten
what is eaten
what anyone wore
while eating it,
nor even,
judging by my recollections
later
who said what
exactly.

THIRTY FIVE

I find that I think of my age again lately
The numbers that name it are with me a lot
Thirty-five, thirty-five, I'm now thirty-five
Good, the coffee is finished…I'm thirty-five.
And later, oh, good, the coffee's still hot
want some / where's a cup / damn, we used
up the cream / there's some milk
life's a dream / still alive / but I'm now thirty-five.

When did Dorothy Parker start writing this shit?
Did she have some good years before
sighing when it
some number or other
came often to mind, salting her days as they grew into
wounds, boozed afternoons
strewing sands quick and deep through
dreamful, sleepless nights?

And I, as I start in my sleep counting sheep in
ironic rhymelets (take my hand, see my lifeline end
after seventeen heroic couplets?)
Do I see only the game, am I blind to the play
If I cleave to my love, will I remember a way
to make love matter?
Or should I see to my garden, cleave solely to self
grow acceptably mad as a hatter?

I see my grandmother; I am my grandmother
huntress at seventy-five.
Antiquing on Saturday, stalking Sheraton

"You know, it keeps me alive!
At home I am loved by a lowboy
his lines and lineage so good!
I am cherished by Chippendale, hot for my Hepplewhite
met and fulfilled by wood!"

My womb is sixty years younger than hers
used only twice (and on offyears)
It's a deal, it's a steal
it's a real
thirty-five year old
badly distressed
Japanese fake
early American cupboard.

EVERYTHING I CAN POSSIBLY THINK OF TO SAY
ON A SUBJECT THAT DOESN'T MATTER BUT ISN'T LIKELY TO GO AWAY
Or
ESSAY ON HOUSEKEEPING

Every woman who's at least partially responsible
for keeping a house clean enough to live in
has got an idea of what's clean enough to live in
and when you go to her house
you're looking at it.

SO I DON'T ASK SOME GOD

Oh, does it *matter* where I appeal?
Does whom I ask really reveal whether I am
still strong
or full of leaks
and dying?
Yes, I think, with an effort of will not needed last year…

it matters.

But I can't ask
me
with the same
getting-rid-of-the-impulse,
leaking the life-ache, cracking
the living-bone of pain
that I get putting
God
in the sentence, (meaning
other than me; *not my fault if I fail*; and
I've asked, now leave me alone.)

So I don't ask some god to
help me remember;
I tell myself to *know;*
nurses brought babies to
Patty Hearst in the hospital.
Had she killed? She could possibly throw
the balance again, for another mother's child.
Still they knew and brought her, in pink and
blue, babies that smiled and beguiled. She had
slept with death, and they feared her.
Then they watched her and sensed her
and brought her the breath of the
smallest, most newly alive.

Nurses "played God."

And they do every day,
and *that* is the way we survive.

ON THE TEMPORARY ABATEMENT OF THE POET'S LEAK PHOBIA WHILE WORKING IN LUIS MAZA'S SCENE SHOP, FORMERLY THE POCKET THEATRE, ON COURTLAND STREET IN ATLANTA

I've never liked leaks.
Or never any but Luis's, there
in the scene shop that's
still, after all, a theatre
of sorts / or types / tripping over
rolled-up tracing paper plans for who
knows what it was, saws, tridents,
two dimensional trolley cars,
yards of tragic wrinkled ambience for Tristan,
Lear's troubled skies,
trellises; Eine Kleine Nacht Musik (later
transposed for the governor's garden party),
encrusted coffee cups,
and glorious rococo Cuban cupids, confused,
possibly, possibly not, by the bar for the winged ballerina,
revolving in breeze from the fans.

The fans / are turned off / when it rains.
Rain sucks its own dark breeze from the sky
sends it through open doors at the back of the shop and
lies restless on the roof,
finds at last its beloved level, drops,
slips down through cracks to invade the space of
yet another, who, Godlike, would not have created this
haven from rain if he'd wanted to work out in it.

An artist missteps, puts a foot on the flat he's painting.
Luis laughs, taps cigarette ash, rubs it in,
grabs a brush, studies…pouts.
"Go fall over there," he says, points to where.
"Not enough to be brilliant once; we must
learn to repeat our effects."
Luis is like that, gradually collects an
adoring crew from a world of exacting papas.

I swear I love the leaks at Luis's,
there, in the scene shop,
guided through hazy polyethylene channels
to fall between flats on the floor like
upside-down fountains to cleverly placed celestial
washtubs / where / further confusing the cupids / you can
fly up and dip in to thin paint—even
rinse your brush in a pinch.

There's something about those bent-over hours
sweating skies onto floors, wringing clouds from sponges
finessing a bird, or two…all the while leaping leaks
that spring from buckets…for they bend you over, the hours
do, and over, then over
till leaks / are fountains / are summer salts.

WHEN THE ROOF LEAKS

Everyone will leave me someday
I think
when the roof leaks.
I wake
dreaming in a waterfall of rocks
and leaves and light—crystal yellowgreen
the one
serigraph I know I'll never make.
My cheek
is dropleted. (Moisture unabsorbed into an oily wall, guarding me
well from love and the heater.)
Awake,
sound survives image. Pattern is obscured in flood. Temptation to
resume the waterfall, call to cottondreamstuff, plug adrenalineleak;
tall Nubians play rosyring around the bush that branches out, then
burns and buckles/ Ceiling paper.
Dawn is not grey, but brown.
Water in a plastic pail has passed through board, closed dark dusty
habitat of upright rusty nails, plaster, lath, dried husks of insect
bodies, sparrow droppings; fossil realms.
Dilute plasma,
it has soaked and ripped its way through paper; poor, thin, parchment
skin of ceiling, roof, my waking lie, protective sky, is done
unglued.
I have, like Chicken Little,
misconstrued.

pale Atlanta dealer / the leaver

I SAW THREE QUEENS

I saw three queens on Thanksgiving
Thanksgiving
Thanksgiving
I saw three queens on Thanksgiving
at a gas station
closed for Thanksgiving.
They wore
wigs and French-fit jeans,
They were
high fashion drag queens.
The first,
vamping with the gas injector
was having his picture taken.
The second,
draped about the hi-test pump
was watching.
The third queen was the photographer from *Blow-up*.
Something moving, down the street,
enlarged, became a woman,
got big eyes. "Oh,"
she said.
"This is going to be in a magazine, isn't it?"
They looked at her.
"Are you all from Rich's?"
They didn't take time to believe her.
"No," said the second,
switching misleadingly to unleaded,
"but we're evil.
Beat it."
She beat it.

BLACK ANDROGENES

She wants to go to Grady Hospital and have her
sex changed *don't let her go she is* everything
female but nothing
familiar about it.
In their one
room she waits for her lover the dealer.
He digs another blackchick, she tells us
other housewives and this time he may not
come back to her
green plants her very clean windows so
she weeps and knots string and
she tells us that she modeled in New York
She has a black
cock
and wants to go to Grady
wants to be a blackchick for her
pale Atlanta dealer
the leaver
Don't
let her go let her don't go don't let her go
she is
everything female but

Light bends sharply through her aura-warp. She's
what she is but
can't see it
wants to be a
don't let her
angeldust…wait…nothing
all those
chicks around
womanwalk…talk…but you
can't tie
nothing down

what will she
why does she
do…want…be…free
warp untangled nest dissolved
aura straightened sex resolved
please don't
can't she see
Grady's public, charity,
and we don't want to be involved
in murder.

MORNING IN COURT

(A Partial Transcript, With Shouting And Excuses)

- George Washington Brown?
- Guilty.
- Homer Mandible?
- Guilty.
- Bessie Lula Mathews?
- Guilty with a excuse.

From the second row of brown benches
pews
I wait
to hear my name
then shout my guilt.

- Harrison Barrymore?
- Not guilty.
- Martin Luthor Pryne?
- Guilty.

Whatever happened to church and state/separation of?
Madelyn Murray, where are you now, when I need you?

- James, come here. Come here, James.
- Yeshyerhonner.
- James, what's all that noise back there?
- Prisoners, Yerhonner.
- Well, James, you go back there and
  tell those prisoners to be quiet.
- Yeshyerhonner.

The room fails to impose.
I was born on a brown bench

I think.
I have always known these rows.

- Zebulon Hershey?
- Here.
- Guilty or innocent?
- What?
- Guilty or innocent?
- Guilty.
- What?
- GUILTY.

None is innocent.
A few are not guilty.
Some are partially guilty,
some guilty with an explanation.
Like most here
I am—guilty—
totally and with no excuses.

- James, come here.
- Yeshyerhonner.
- James, those prisoners are still
  laughing back there. What's
  going on in there, James?
- I don't know, Yerhonner. I'll go
  see.
- Yes, James, would you do that?
- Yeshyerhonner.

I am at home here.
We are a family.
There is some fear here
but no social unease.

- Ashida Tambaki?
- Guilty.
- Grace Zambrowski?

I could say

                              - Here

gain a moment
during

                              - Guilty or innocent?

but God's here too
—or as here as Yerhonner—
and these two laugh
at temporizers.

                              - Grace Zoobruski?
                              - Guilty.

Besides,
I prefer offering guilt as
immediate proof of existence.
It seems cleaner...
more initiated...
certainly more true.

VICARIOUS TAURUS

Elaine's tired of starving.
Her brains and roses start to curl
after just so many weeks and years
of never having enough jack to buy food,
buy paint and canvas, find time to
sit back and wonder how to live today,
say stick it to a rude old world.
And that's crucial—that last one.

She's parading it now. To music.
Got herself in top shape—except for
tits, maybe. Guy there says she'll have to
fix that, if she expects to work till forty.
Little slit, pull it up and over,
tuck it, stitch, that's it. No sweat, he says.
She says fuck it. Don't want to work till
forty. Dance my ass through this summer,
make some cash, paint it, write poems about it.
Yeah.

Hmm.
Me too—that last one.

TODAY I FOUND THE PHOTOGRAPH OF A LONG DEAD FRIEND AMONG THE PERSONAL ADVERTISEMENTS IN A CURRENT ISSUE OF A SWINGER'S MAGAZINE

Is it you, my friend,
posthumously swinging out there in the
coy and shrunken buttocks world of
whips,
"French, Greek and Roman Arts" and
garter belts with black net stockings?

Is it true, my friend,
arduously preparing the notice of your death
in ten point type, that you were dying to
swing, and then you died, and then you
swang?
And now you've swung, my friend, refused to
hang black crepe on your velvety ass,
rung the bell of non-renaissance in the
advertisement section of a swingers magazine to
screen prospective partners without undue
preliminaries such as bored you in the past,
have you at last found how to sing, as you once
sang before the swong was finally swung?

TO TOWER WATCHERS

And there will be masses of mass murders,
Mister, and many will be for love.
For sympathy and passion,
world disgust and shame
in name of altruism's bloody glove
(and some, by God, for fame.)
But blame it on the guns, old man,
or blame it on a tumor; or tell us
all that we're to blame, and never
heed the rumor that the seed was sown
in every mind
two thousand years ago.
Remember?
"Do not question why, but
know…(ye)
somehow, that you are your brother's keeper."

Sit quietly, friend. Bolt all your doors
and hope that too much logic will not be
unlocked by madness.

THE TEACHING IS LEARNED

and the teaching is learned
and the learning is taught   (REPEAT 3 TIMES)

and
haven't you all been my teachers?
and haven't I been yours?
or is it only that insanity is a communicable
disease
easier than love / to contract?
I am a teacher
but I teach what I have learned, and
the problem is / how not to teach / what I was too
dumb
not to stick around / long enough / to learn.
(DRUM UP)

take a step
then
take it back
build a bridge
then
break it.
find a way
through the dark
love it light
then
lose it.   (DRUM OUT)
and the teaching is learned
and the learning is taught   (DRUM UP)

do me good
hold me tight
say you love me
then
start a fight. (DANCE SEQUENCE W/O WORDS)

and the teaching is learned
and the learning is taught
I don't say to my love now
what you said to hurt me
I don't do what you did to wound
my love and I have learned new ways
and they are sound
proof to echoes of the days
when I was learning all you knew.

and, Daddy,
since you did what you knew you shouldn't
I shall do what I swore I wouldn't
and turn my skill to making bumper stickers;
SUICIDE IS CATCHING.   (DRUM UP)

take a step
then
take it back
build a bridge
then
break it
find a way
through the dark
love it light
then
lose it.

make a stair
make it strong
make it wind / ing
make it long
in / vi / ting
ain't it fine
and
it's only ours
love
yours and mine.
post a sign / on the stair
down's the right way
up's not fair.

WORD DANCER'S DILEMMA

(poem to be danced to jazz; "Bitches' Brew" by Miles Davis)

Music / send me into movement.
I hear music and I
go to town.

I whiz past glass walls…
stop
tentatively dressing my bones in what is
or is not
appropriate.

I lurk
squarely
on the concrete rooves
of rooms that house the sewers.

Lots going on down there
Got lots to see down there
More down there
than
meets
the eye.

Deliberation…here
is no more than
summoning
en / er / gy
Decision…comes
through my ear
shoots to muscle
seeps through tissue

Music says "GO."
Later I say
yes
or no.

Music sends me into movement
but WORDS send me…you know…
words gotta go through my
head
first.

OH INDIA

Do I dare to sing of freedom
and as hope 'hind progress lags
say I do not bow to elephants
and have never cared for flags?

Do I dare to pay my taxes
while explaining to my young
that good's not wrought by axes
and that to hold one's tongue
when evil rules
is deadly sport
a game
that's never won?

And when they listen to the medley
'tis of thee, say can you see, and one which
staunchly swears their fealty to all which
reeks of perjury and power lust and force…

what then?

Do I dare forget all fact
advise take sides among the knaves
wait for those who know to act
pray new life emerge from caves?

THE CAGE

You enter the cage, leaving open
the door

You show her meat
she leaves her seat
and she comes wagging in to eat

You sweetly greet her
with your treat

Repeat repeat:

Oh man, oh man, but ain't she sweet
Come eat this meat, come dig my treat
Ain't it some treat to be called sweet
You're some sweet treat, babe, eat my meat,
babe, sweet sweet sweet
I kiss your feet, babe, your sweet feet
Come on repeat now, ain't she sweet, I've said it
twice now,
ain't she sweet come on repeat, more sweetly
sweet now
ain't she sweet…

And she believes how, she be's sweet now
She eats the meat now, eats your meat, it's just her
meat
It's her meat now…

and it's her cage now

and you leave, closing the door.

From a Time in My Life

MANTRA

Let me tell you something, little girl;
you're not me.
And let me tell me something, little girl;
I'm not you.
Now.
Maybe we can both grow up.

FROM A TIME IN MY LIFE

I

Marion waits till her daddy wakes up
(on his chosen sleep-late days)
then she jumps on the big bed
andtakesthepillowslipsoffasfastasshecan
(and sometimes she throws the pillows out the window!)
She climbs into one pillowslip
and pulls it up to her neck
and the other one goes
right over her head—like this!
(She's as supple as a young willow.)
What are you?
asks her mommy.
A ghost?
No, no, NO! laughs Marion.
I'm a PILLOW!

II.

CONNECTIONS

Child's brush leaded with watercolor
                              gray
sky on the window.
Child-tensed fingers, table-paper
                                    spread
branches lacing cloud and bluer yonder.
Robins round their nest both
                              building
cocky red and damp blue fantasies
of paint and straw, laughing twigs
and chirping, playing, darting thinking
ecstasies of work.

III

Marion has brand new sandals.
Her toes are separated and her ankles
neatly banded, and the buckles are
for doing and for doing and for doing..

And make my popsicles freeze NOW,
Mommy.

They have been waited for, these
sandals,
and the summerytime they promised
has arrived with dampish tendrils near the ears.

And some fears...

Beautiful, beautiful brown eyes,
I'll never love

Don't want blue eyes any MORE, Mommy.

Wash the dark off the windows, Mommy.

She walks on Italo-American air
spiced tenderly with gingerly (not
cinnamon or basily) all
three year old cautious
not to dusty nor to darken her soles.

IV

NOTE
TO HELEN
(an eleven year old weaver)
Today's been slow
I filled some holes in boards
The van won't go

No one came to Richard's show
except the critics
I got rejected for a job
I never asked for, so,
Helen,
won't you make your weaving grow?

V

LULLABY

I'll sing you an elephant
I'll sing you a bear
I'll sing you a rabbit who's hiding
from a fox who is no longer there.

I'll sing you a turtle dove
I'll sing you a whale
I'll sing you a black and white puppy dog
who is barking and chasing his tail

I'll sing you a killer whale
I'll sing you another dove
I'll sing you two prickly porcupines
who want most of all to find love

I'll sing you a kangaroo
I'll sing you a mouse
I'll sing you a snail who is tired
of dragging around his own house

I'll sing you an antelope
I'll sing you a cow
I'll sing you a sleepy baby
who is closing her eyelids now

VI

SIXTEEN

He won't
look me in the eyes
she tells me.
And I am her mother.
I jump into tears before I can think.
My God, I say.
I once fell in love with a man in a bar.
He'd returned my look. I felt met.
I used to tell your father I'd leave him in
a minute for a man who'd talk to me in bed.
No, she says.
He's OK on the lovey-dove stuff.
It's when we talk.
Just talk.
He can't…he
just
won't

look.

CHILD FALLEN FROM A MOVING CAR

Terror of the open
cyclone cellar door in an
outward swerving,
soaring prairie house

glimpse of Winkie witch heels, silver

dust, dead,
now, though only-
Sweet Wizard!
no more than
Oz-wicked.

GIRL CHILDREN

Girl children are our sisters too.
Our daughters, our friends' daughters,
all girl children are our sisters
as we
and they
are sisters to each other.

When my work is so important as to
constantly exclude them…
…my daughtersisters…

Then that work is too important for me
too important for love
too important for growth.

Let others emulate the male's stupid
shunning
of his young…
…to find himself
to achieve importance…

I choose to try to be stronger
to do more
to do it my way.

I can't
help it
if our grandmothers were strong in
wrong
ways
and for sad
reasons.

Crazies

BALLAD OF THE AX

Walked in swinging an ax, he did
Spit tobacco juice on the floor
Didn't say much
Opened the door and walked in
Made neither threats nor promises.

She needed to ascertain his mood
understand the motives that moved him
He was rude in neither
word nor look
but his body language was grim

He hummed some, and he smiled a little
as he strolled to the cellar door
She suspected he wished to chop up the plumbing
that he'd botched up the year before.
Don't bother, it's fixed already, she said

trying to take his plumber's tool
But he was no fool and he grabbed her hair
and lifted her off the floor
A friend came in and called the police
who arrived half an hour later

He was gone by then. Now the women share
blood and stitches between them.
The house is cold
Plumbing's gone again
There's wood—but the ax went off with the policemen.

CRAZIES

I.
You say he's burned all the beehives,
taken them out into the back yard
and built a bonfire
to heaven
threatening
even
the telephone wires?

And now he's back from a
runaway
trip
to Florida
where he sat under the tree where
something
happened to him with his sister and had
dreams about your
daughter?

And now he fears
the bees will finally come
from Sears
and have no place to live?

And now
he hears
you don't want him back again
and wishes
you did?

II.
He beat you up so bad you ran out of the house
naked,
and then he beat you up on the front porch until a
neighbor came out and looked at you from her
porch, and
then he shouted at her excitedly that he'd caught
you
with another man
and she nodded
and went back inside.
And you screamed that he lied
but she stayed inside.

III.
Your daughter is crying and hates you
and she says you've misunderstood.
He brings presents, and he's really a nice man
and he touches her where it feels good.

Hey, I know, you say, and—I'm sorry,
and, Baby, it's hard to explain,
but grown-ups who need little children
to touch
are not loving, but hiding from pain
that they feel, from…
well, it's really hard to explain.

I KNOW he feels pain, she tells you.
She cries, that's why I hold him so tight,
'cause the room where he sleeps when he comes here's
darkscary, and he needs me right by him all night.

He told me I'd better not tell you,
that you never would understand it.
We guess names for his penis, like Dennis,
and Lollipop, and Big-boy, and Hot-job,
and once it got big when I fanned it.

When I start to guess
he feels bad, feels like dying,
until I guess right, and he laughs.
But, you know what? His penis starts crying.

IV.
You say he shakes you
and wakes you
and diddles you dumb
and if you forget
and you start to come
he goes
away ?

And you know
that he knows
that this is the place
and this is the way
he can make you pay
and pay
and pay.

And today you explained
that you felt abused;
almost—used—
and used is a hard word;
it made him cry.
But he wanted to please you,
He wanted to try.
He said, I love you, Honey.
So you swallowed your tears
and the rest of his
till fear was no more in your chest than a wiggle
that wobbled
a little,
as you strained and floated and sweated and
groaned.
And you heard his sound, and you thought he'd
moaned.
But he hadn't. He's started to giggle.
Hee, hee, hee, he said. He was amused.
You should see your face. It's so funny.

V.
You say he wants you for himself now
told all your friends to go away
won't even let you see your family
says he thinks your mother's gay?

VI.
Your mother says

> What do you mean, your doctor's crazy?
> What are you so upset about?
> He thinks he's God? Well, that I doubt.
> Look, find another one, don't be so lazy.
>
> He has you whitely paper-gowned
> but it's turned around.
> Your back is bare, his nurse takes care
> She KNOWS your cunt's in front,
> but this is how he likes it.

You wait,
wondering how the man will
manage.
One thing sure; this
man
was not brought up by
missionaries.
He enters quickly
does not smile
stares for a second at your blank, white front
proceeds
to solve
its riddle.
Catching your eye,
he holds it while
he rips you
down
the middle.
You wait,
wondering how this is supposed to make you
feel.
Thrillingly violated?
What else?
To bitch
or not to bitch
at being
paper
raped; THAT
is the question.
To trust
or not to trust
the impulse
to imply
that despite a certain style
the man lacks
sanity.

VII.
Methyl ethyl keytone was his aura,
sitting there,
lotus legged on the coffee table
pouring more, more and
more
mineral spirits from a gallon can
to drench the thick, drab army overcoat

he wore, to drench,
well,
any animal spirits in him,
to drench,
well,
the pack of matches in his
pocket.
And you sat on the floor beside him
crying no
no
while your friend stripped him
naked and put him in the bath
tub, where he sat, again,
playing in the water, looking at
her from time to time, as
she washed him. Slyly,
he asked her if she
had seen your
face.
Triumphantly; did you see her *face*?
Took you a year, didn't it,
to understand those bravely sodden
matches?
Thank God,
you said,
for a goddam year
or more,
he poured so much spirit on his
soggy soul,
he prayed so much Buddhist bullshit on his
sad, sodden self—
he wet the matches.

VIII.
You say he shot at you
from the top of the stairs
and later you found the bullet
at the bottom of the stairs
against the wall
in a shoe?

What did you do?
Oh. He says he didn't mean
to hit
you.
he meant
to hit
the shoe.
Hmmm.
You think it's true?

Well, I don't know what he is.
But I'll tell you what he's
not.
He's not
a bad shot.

IX.
And when you put the phone back down
like the cover on a burnt-black
pot
or
the toy chest lid on a
sleeping child
whom you'd flashed
for a moment
was dead

or like
hanging
up
a phone

you noticed him
hating down at you there
on the floor
where you'd sat
half an hour
trying hard to convince
an old
virgin

lover
to clean up one wrist
and not to cut
another
and he said
tossing socks
in a box
sounding exactly
like socks
that you'd rolled
being tossed
in a cardboard
box
"I'm leaving, you know, like I'm gonna split. Like every
hard-dick son-of-a-bitch between here and California thinks
he can call you up in the middle of the night."

And the truest thing
you knew
to say
was that you'd always had trouble with
similes.

HUNG

he squeezes his love through a knothole
he sends his force down a drain
he spends his strength on keyholes and laundry chutes
swearing never to leave this house again.

he smoothes splinters with his tongue
works long and hard to form a tiny erect clitoris in the
rough floorboard, keeping an air return happy with his toes.
lover-like, spread-eagle, he joy-labors to make a mingle of
him and house. He really doesn't want to leave the house again.

hung like Michelangelo, he performs ecstatic miracles for the
chimney and the overhead sockets, sweats soot, sparks of
rare and homely lust,
hoping
he'll never have to leave this house
again.

Trying to Refabricate My Life

THREE TIMES RAIN

I
VIEW FROM THE ATTIC - AFTER THE STRIKE
(1979, Atlanta, just before leaving for Los Angeles)

Over the kudzu, houses away, a man sings.
Rain fills the air between.
This is the room I built for myself.
Since I'm going away
I suppose I could say that
now I never will use it.
Or I could say
I'm using it now.
Well, I am.
I'm using it now.
Can I separate myself from love for that much joy,
at least?

I want a huge black notebook like Steinbeck had
to write EAST OF EDEN and his editor a letter for a year.
Don't need—don't want anyone to give it to me.
Want to buy it myself.
I will.
I'll buy it myself.

Mornings after plays are vicious.
Deserve orgies, but there's never the energy.

The stage where Alice never lived is gone.
I helped destroy it.
That seemed the least I could do.
Oh, bullshit! She lived.
She lived a little.
Possibly as much as many.
Whatever that means.

Means I'm trying to give myself a break
for a change. So what
if it leans a bit toward foolishness, the
silly wisdom I see others needing
and generally spare myself.

first
highway sign

BEWARE ! TRAINED FOOLISHNESS !
WILL ATTACK ON SIGHT !
(YOU MIGHT GET BY, SOME
CHANCY NIGHT, BUT HEED !
TAKE CARE ! DOWN THIS ROAD
LIVE GOD, RIGHT THINKING, &
OTHER QUESTIONS OF SLIGHT COMFORT.)

THE MGMT.

The singer stops. Timid heaven weeps afresh.

II

Where are the rains of yesteryear?
New Orleans rains were pulsing things.
God ate much and badly there—
gasses churned and organs thumped.
Results on earth were good for birth
death, decay, and drowning of all
small, dry-spirited mammals.
Children that lived grew up damp.
It was good for them.
Their breasts got large—
they learned to catch on quicker.

Wooden map drawers swelled, became recalcitrant, unpredictable.
A young biology teacher caught a breast in one, twice.
Same breast, same drawer.
Both times, her eyes were startled,

And we, concerned and happy.
Happiness clouded by concern at first,
then concern overshadowed by
rampant joy.

Concern and joy
joy and concern;
at length these blended
in the mind to form some
essence of the time.

Surely, we all remember?
Surely, none has forgot?

*second
highway sign*

MEMORY SAVES

Imperative to clear up this matter.
Formal poll—high school reunion; but
how to ask the question?

What do you remember best, about
Miss Putnam's fine long breasts?
Alternate: What's the first painful thing that
comes to mind when you think, "biology charts"?

In Atlanta there is too much rain
from time to time, but
never enough for premature development.
Or swellings of any kind,
beyond those requiring no
imagination for desiring.

III

Los Angeles, 1987

Actual thunder.
Rare rain in la la land.
The poem can continue.

Rehearsal cancelled—not for rain but
arriving Argentinians.
Thunder.

The text will be read in Spanish and English,
alternating languages.
I will speak English, but today
I stare at the Spanish.
Under pressure
it comes occasionally clear.

Thunder.

"I speak little Spanish," I can now say
to the visiting playwright. And
"My conversation is limited
to the vocabulary of desire."

He will understand less
than I of what I say.
Or more.
Oh, thunder!

PRIME TIME

Eighty dollars worth of news today from home.
That's prime time. That's Hollywood.

Sometimes I have to leave and let things happen.
It's been too long since the last time.

How do they stand my being there
keeping things together forever?

Of course all I have to worry about here
is how to pay for being away

and remembering to keep the door closed
so the cat can't piss in my boots.

VENTURA STAR

Today they honked at me on the freeway.
(And get this; I'm *doing* sixty!)

A Colt with miles to spare on
either side comes up behind
whinnies, and passes,
completing his point by regaining his lane dangerously
close to my front end.
I honk back, make
that gesture I love so much when
Italians do it.

Moments later, he's gone.
I watch for him,
wishing I had a P.A. system,
and see, suddenly, no
car on the freeway not
red or rust or orange.

My little silver Honda shivers.
Visions, we think, are where you find them.

Then out of the blue hills behind
comes canary yellow; some
monstrous make, godcar,
horizontal fin gleaming like the
misplaced, offhand crown it is,
jutting out like a bad bustle
from last period picture show
the actors try not to remember.

It streaks by, swerves, and weaves
the visible world together.
Ventura star, too fast
to be furious with anyone.

TRYING TO REFABRICATE MY LIFE

Trying to refabricate my life
in a Los Angeles apartment.
My friend has found coffee with chickory
at a supermarket.
Cream was easy.
Sugar she's forgotten to throw out after the
wayward visit of some dangerous aunt.
So I have that.
Thanks to my friend, her remembering
and her forgetting,
I can have coffee.

She has therapy today.
I stay with a cat, who,
according to his mistress, is retarded—
believes himself a turtle.
I can see that.
He sat like that last night
on the arm of the couch.
This morning I find him gracious. Showing
companionship,
when, for all I know, I may need it most, he
urinates pristinely
in the wash basin.
We tinkle together,
he longer, gloating
over the superiority of the male bladder.
Signaling an end to his ablutions
he scratches invisible grains of porcelain sand
to cover
invites me
to go right ahead and brush my teeth.
In his absence I inspect the basin.

His aim is nicer
than others I have known; still,
I pass, my own absolutes
dark
as a cat's.

I've done the dishes,
broken a cup, cut my finger on it.
A trail of darker drops of blood is dry.
The turtle-cat won't touch it,
though earlier
it glistened.
I should find washing machines.
A key has been left on the phonograph.
If I went out
I could get back in.

Catching the sun
in a glass bowl
is a Hollywood tangerine.

NATURAL FORCES

Crying over you
and the bad hair day you
have made of my life
lately
I drip tears onto my
newly made-up lower eyelashes
my chalky cheeks.
The make-up artist seems not to notice.
He daubs and blots without a word,
repairs my water damage. Does it
again and again, as this is needed;
knows, in his vast experience, that
if he stops and
waits for me to finish,
floods will come.

He is earlier man,
simpler, older, wiser.
He accommodates himself to natural forces
without useless rancor.
But you and I are rivers and seas,
rising.
We push the many dams and dykes,
swell to
overflow the streams of one another.
We are the suns,
and we are the moons,
and we are the tides,
and we are the winds.
We seem to find the pulse of constant level
just about as often as the world does.

THE CLOSENESS OF WOLVES

I'm asking you now, tonight, to tell me.
About the wolves.
The tape you play of their howlings.

Everything stops when you play that tape.
The house goes dead.
I can think only of your listening.

Tonight I feel frightened, lonely.
Those sounds are like nothing else, really.
Memory rises; there's a fire, and all around there are
wolves.

When they howl, are they lonely?
Other wolves answer…
Their howls reach out…touch.

What are you doing tonight, my love?
Reliving, like me, old dangers
and fears of the closeness of wolves?

Or have you become wolf?
Fierce,
alone,
forgetting
that wolves do something about it?

THESE BRIEF AND SPASTIC COUPLINGS WE HAVE NOW

These brief and spastic couplings we have now
are not what I had in mind.
So I will not have them there.
You allow them to mean almost nothing,
so for me they must mean less than that.
For me they must not even exist.
I must retreat into this
respect
you say you lack from me.
You will have that, and so
some measure of my hopes—
the ones for you, that others share, who know you.

Will you have from me only what they give?
Go back to them, then. Find the courage to leave me.
Go back to where all your longtime friendly strangers live.

ANHEDONIA

It seems I shrink these days
…from everything, and,
in consequence,
absolutely.
I grow small
I grow small
I soon shall find pleasure in nothing at all,
at this rate.

Even weight loss worries me.

So much is now gone
I can't see a gain
when my ass gets
smaller
numbers
stare
at my face, you
don't, anymore, I go insane, and
nothing hangs in the balance.

ONE MEDIUM MAN

I used to go to movies
Then I watched the world
through the medium
of television
Once of course I read the papers
an occasional novel
cried

Recently I tried
all these at once
They lied
dangerously
at odds with me &
one another
I OD'd &
moved to California
became pure

I'm saner now

I wear sunglasses
At work at play
in bed at home
I see my world
in monochrome
& float the freeways
stride the city sidewalks

ANGEL MIRROR

This mirror,
high on the wall not
cracked in the quake
- just over the head of a
  tarnished bed too
  creaky to fuck on -
is empty.

Poems

QUEEN OF THE WASTE STREAM

Joan Edwards is my hero.
She is the new Director of Integrated Solid Waste
Management in Los Angeles, and she
makes me feel better
about
Integrated Solid Waste Management in Los Angeles
now that she's the Director
of it.

Joan Edwards was in New York before,
where she figured out what to do about their garbage,
and now she's here,
figuring out what to do about ours.

Ours is tougher, she says, and I'm really glad.
We're tougher than you, New York, and
so is our garbage.

Joan, the ways I have felt about garbage
up until now, are, in chronological order:

> 1. No way at all, really. Nothing.
> 2. Guilty. And resentful. Resentfully guilty.
> 3. Existentially hopeless.

You are my hero, Joan, because you have made me feel
less hopeless.

Is it possible that there could be a correlation
between attitudes toward garbage and attitudes
toward life?
Oh, Joan, how could there not be?
Joan Edwards has guessed that glass can be
used in asphalt, instead of sand and stone.

New Yorkers are already driving over their old
Yoo Hoo bottles, crack vials, broken bud vases,
pickle jars and perfume stoppers. She has to come
up with a lot more of these ideas and then talk
people into using them.
She has to talk people into buying garbage.
Which is done all the time, of course, but
labeling's so important, and Joan won't really
have that going for her. Until it catches on,
of course. And I think it will.

Still, my first dream about "The Waste Stream,"
as she calls it, was a nightmare. I was drowning
in this mighty river of shit. Which is
partly why I really wish the *L.A. Times*
wouldn't call Joan "The Waste Queen."
And why I worry about Joan's dreams.
I do.
And I have other worries.

Like, if Joan picks up all the empty bottles,
what then will be the use
of homeless people and drug addicts and other
unneeded, poor, but slightly enterprising children?

And what about this, Joan?
What about people who *need* their garbage,
who save it, in case they need it, but really
so they can watch it and walk through it, or
talk to it, or just sense it in there, in the closets,
everyday? Will they feel free to keep on doing
this, feel free to contribute very little to The
Waste Stream, really, until they die? Will you
then and only then go on in and feed the cats
and sort it all out for them into two room-
sized bundles for recycling day?
    One small bathroom-sized bundle
    of metal, glass, and plastic
    containers, and

One medium bedroom-sized bundle
of newspapers, magazines, and
corrugated boxes, and

another pile,
a bundle already,
smaller,
tied with twine,
which say,

"Congratulations, Alice Bundy, you have just won $2,000,000!"
and
"Alice Bundy, we want YOU in our club!"
and
"You are being sent a new ElDorado, Alice Bundy, so read
further!"

from DETAILS OF DOMESTIC SCIENCE-FICTION (I)

If a square cloth is placed
on a round table
then a white throated kitten may
claw his way up the fringe towards
one person sitting at an inner apex
of angles
of cloth.
The kitten will be upside down
the person will be rightside up
according to a view of things no
more than a few inches above
sea level.

from DETAILS OF DOMESTIC SCIENCE FICTION (II)

When tree sex scums
a window sill
this condition is best remedied by
musings
long leanings
out the window
while being gently fucked from behind.
In this organic method
of windowsill cleaning
elbows are employed
grease has its place
and all materials involved
inescapably
ultimately
biodegradable.
Be creative!
Variations are feasible
limited only by imagination, immediately
available furniture
and the size of the
window
aperture.

PICTURE POEM FROM CAPOTE—TO A YOUNG, ADMIRING AUTHORESS

```
                Up
             on the
         church steeple
        highest shelf of
    a blue corner cupboard

        Dutch blue

    stands a white cock

        Alabaster.

    A turtle, green and Mexican
      mottled, sits beneath him;
    though one toe is broken, so
      he must be useful and not
      merely              watched.
                            s
          His               l
       heavy iron            a
      body perspires          n
    and re-decorates a book    t
            as it                s

    against him. See him there.
    Their order on the shelves is
    blackface wrong. When turtle
    sweat a soul will swear...the
    whitest highest cock will not
    pride                      long.
```

PACHYDERM WHORE

The pachyderm whore is angry now.
She's gone and won't be back.

rolled up her night lamp and the candles
for her gum plates in her mattress, tied
around with stretched pink rubber douche
bag hose and wrote on all the walls fuck
you baby and walked right out the door
and won't be back. Left a present on the
table but baby that's the last you'll see of her because
she's gone and mad and won't be back.

Lumbering down the street encumbered, loaded
down with all she owns and less,

and if you were among the few who knew the
great gray folds of swaying skin beneath
the black and orchid dress, you heard again
the blaring horns of elephants calling—
wished you dared go home and smash the small
black scratchy disk she'd left with you
because you'd begged for it (for laughs)
before you knew that from now on no more
than she could you "do it" to another music.

(less than success with girls who cared
to be compared with pussycats)

But hello, Ellie, smile the men and street
kids as she passes, hello, Ellie, moving on
again? Among them is the elephant child—
took ten full months to bear him—she scoops him
up onto her pack where he clutches the mattress
with all four monkey feet and stares into
the face of the black African slave of a night
lamp and wishes to hell that elephants were not
so easily wounded.

Lemon Cake Pie

(for Penny)

How many great aunts kissed
without complaining

How many marble troves lost
How many jacks left spinning

How many babies minded
pianos practiced, homeworks done
rooms cleaned up
all deemed entertaining

How many fortunes tossed
How many dreams invaded
weddings attended
funerals unevaded

So as not to miss
not to be denied
not the sight nor the smell
nor the sound of the name
of the dream of the love
of the very idea
of a lemon cake pie.

SOME BOOKS FOR YOUR BIRTHDAY

(for John)

There are maybe miles of books
in the bookstore, shelves and aisles,
covers, words and faces;
wood, meadow, subway entrance, super
market maze of sustenance and dross.

Miles and miles of books in the bookstore

Has some nocturnal bookworm,
heavy with insomnia, ever
dragged them out,
end to end,
laid them out to see?

Miles and miles of books in the bookstore, but
which for you
and which for me?

I make my face into your face,
my eyes into your eyes;
I'll walk along the subway now and see
which windows in the trains reflect you…
But you come too, your face and eyes,
and height
and hands
There is no being you, only being
by you as you bend to me, stare with me into the
unzinked mirror of some desperate gum machine
unable,
unstabled by the roar of trains, to
tell us from each other.

POET

Antithesis of ease personified,
you are a paraplegic on stilts
a spastic deer,
a sensitive in perpetual shock.
We talk. You
stutter; awareness curdles on your words.
Sentences slow and convolute, cocoon,
flutter into apologies.
Flecks of wit, unnoticed, dot your chin,
your tongue-in-cheek is bitten—bleeds.
Forever rebelling, your body screams,
reeking your armpits; it would green
your teeth, if it could.

But your teeth
and eyes
are clean
and I love you
want you
with me
in some bed
for hours…
face unfurled…

Then, I think, you would probably remember
the time…and that you had things to do.

SPECIAL DAY FOR THE BLIND

There was a special day for the blind
at the museum; an eight hour celebra-
tion of someone's sense that when one
sense must work for two - this ought to
be permitted. The blind entered early
on their special day. Thousands came,
by nine. Few left before five, and of
these, most were infiltrators, poseurs
who saw as well as you or I, drawn by
promises of touch. Each had—for it
had taken—much "brass" to come, (mo-
tives, of course, differed,) but soon
they quailed; intimidated somehow, by
illumination; intimations, sliding into
minds; the blind knew brass—its trumpet
smell, alloyed unelemental color, green feel of
myriad patinas. Righteousness sickened, and died.
The unblind withdrew (by noon)...but this is not their story...
The true blind stayed to plague the guards, whose
lives seemed harder then, than they'd ever been;
forbidden to hinder the unthinkable, invited,
in fact, to aid these gropers past ropes
whose lines defined, till now, sin or an
absence of it. Two guards were old and
died of heart attacks within the week.
The rest discussed it hotly with their
wives—but shakily—torn between twin
virtues of pity and indignation...and
always, til memory forgave, the vision:
meaten knuckles glissing grave abysses
cleaving cheek & cheek, cheek & eye
and groin & thigh; all unashamed and
thirsty finger suck of dust from stone
hollows; all quest for any evidence of
sight; soft vigil for evidence of man.

EDUCATIONAL T.V.

(Dialogue Between A Museum Curator And A Businessman)

Mild eyed man,
museum keeper,
squirming in his chair
at the mention of
Picasso. Exciting!

Yes,
he's just like other people onlymoreso.
He hears everything,
he remembers everything,
he knows my son's entire course of
study—graduate and undergraduate,
you know, yes, I have the lobster
shell he decorated without ever
seeming once to notice what he did—
just like breathing with him, don't
you know?
Regalar waiter's delight.

And Jacqueline…?

is always there. She sits outside
his studio door all night, waiting
lest he need some thing…

Yes, cross my legs and
bright my curatoreyes,
she certainly is a
guardian angel to him,
isn't she?

When he learned what work it was that
I had bought of his—he doesn't know
the titles that we give them—he went
off into ecstasies about it to the
bookstore owner there—as if the painting
had been done by quite another ha, ha—
as if he were not speaking of his own.
Would you like to come with me and visit
he said then. No, you've been so nice
to us already—and his eyes were sad—
I like you both so much he said—he
said he liked us both so much and asked
us to come on, but we had intruded
enough, we thought, and so we left

Such an addition to our understanding of his work
itself, wish we could go on indefinitely however

DE RE ARS POETIQUE

On the assumption, Marie, Dame, that
nothing would be duller than some
reasonable pedantry,
  (patient, mild,
   some essay attempting to
   encompass all,
   temperate,
   the only part disdained
   or wrong proclaimed
   that art that never
   left the heart for paper,
   and then not necessarily; fairily
   brimming with judiciousness,
   cool,
   impassionate, impossible
   to write, more painful still
   to read),

I calm myself.
The shrill, dogmatic path is mine, and
I shall trip it thinly, as have others.
This way is clear to me, it's mine, and
if I shriek it at you hotly, then I
risk no hateful cries of treasonable
sedition.
Hail, brothers;
Horace, Boileau, Vida, Pope…
we wrest within tradition.

But then begone and damn you all,
Notre Dame included. I've
named your muses, called your ruses,
and I have no other use for you at all.
I say this; I say SAY

SOMETHING.
Say it so you'll care you said it later,
while you eat your dinner.
Make a mold of imperfection,
cast a seal, and stamp it on
each sheet of a printer's perfect ream.
Five hundred and sixteen perfect chances
you'll have then,
to ward off witches
and devils of dullness.
Go a HEAD, stick your NECK out,
put your FOOT in it,
make it throb like a blue THUMB,
and if it sticks out,
well it's sore, man, and at least it isn't
hidden in your metaphorical pocket.

NO WAY TO WRITE

There was
no way to write, when I stopped smoking.
Where were thoughts to come from…air?
Where was the stare of one eye winking,
watching the risk, the seeming dare, that's
really only a trade;
there are dreamings lost and dreamings gained here,
for payments must be made.

(And the tip of my thumb's a living blister
matches catch festering, can't resist. There's
payment due here, and must be made.)

I need
this think-code never dreamed by Morse
of shapes of fingers, wrist turns, tappings,
two-way sappings of filtered force.

Fire and ash.
Fire and ash.
There's my muse.

NATIONAL GEOGRAPHIC POEM #3
SHY COMMUNICATION FROM A PORTION OF THE MID-OCEANIC RIDGE TO HER SISTERS, WHO HAVE NOT YET ALL BEEN FOUND

I am the East Pacific Rise at 21° North.
Inside, I am all atremble.
In my cracks, molten magma wells up,
meets cold seawater and solidifies
into a contorted landscape of black lava.

Of what this means for me we will not speak
—except to say
contortions abound
—to add; awareness—that
this does not make one unique.

Have we not all seen seaworms wafting cheek to cheek
with tideless deepsea currents, branching out, but
fastened, always,
anchored down at warm spots,
which are what we provide?

Thighs so deep in Earth I do not know them, my sighs
escape me hot with pity…for me, for the worms…
gutless wonders feeding on my warmer waters.
Sometimes I dream of elephants, hear them, and the sounds of
small birds who are, at least, their friends, are of some use,
provide some service; at times, see green.

How do I know of these: green, birds, elephants, sound?
My worms are red, the only strong color
to survive these depths.

Echoes. I wish they would not reach me. I wish I were
a seaworm, bulging with blood, turgid, swaying, anchored,
asleep.
The echoes never wake the worms.
They slumber, thrive, and cannot drown.

DROPPING THE BOOKS

The books are in bookshelves in the hall.
Only there.
Not only there.
Some larger ones are
elsewhere.
But aside from elsewhere
all the books are in the hall.
That was the deal
when I bought this house.
I would no longer live with
books in every room as
sole décor.
I would live
with as many books
as could fit in the hall
alphabetized by author
from ceiling to floor.

Every two years, too
many just-read books have been
jammed into spaces above the properly
shelved. They must be reunited,
like the far flung offspring of prolific sperm donors,
with their siblings
alphabetically
or shoved alone
into company that is,
at least, alliterative.
But first

it is time for the dropping of the books.

My sturdy library ladder comes out from its place under the portrait of my
father—even though it was my mother with the books—
and I move it down the hall, far left,
and climb to the top
to the A's.
Not as many "A"s as you would think. There are four times as many "B"s.
There is no more space.
Lots of books must go. None of these A's or B's must go, but some
can go, and that is good enough.
So they go, dropped
down flat to the wooden floor.
By the time my ladder has
reached the end of the long, narrow hall
the floor is covered with A through F,
and the books must be gathered
and boxed
before I start back
culling from the opposite wall.

I am not Alexandria,
nor was meant to be.
Others, now,
must deal with them all,
making sure for lifetimes that none
is lost, until
they all are.

AS THOUGH

You made me stay
but you put me by

How did I stand for it
I should have walked away
when you wouldn't let me look at you.
You weren't shy
not really

As though any word
any look between us
could as well be lies
and only deeds
only time
only faithfulness
would matter.

And they have.

But I needed to drown
in your eyes
eyebrows
lashes
lips.

That certain smell where
the hairs sprout from your chest
not completely pleasant
that smell
but it was odd and it was
interesting and it was
yours
and I loved it.
Clay.
That's what it was.
I remember.

FRIDAY, AUGUST 18, 2006

Wonder of wonders
there is no war
anywhere.

World calm
peace unbreached.
Unimpeached,

breathing deep,
leaders seem to join
the nation

contemplating
more important matters.
Who killed the child

whose tawdry photos rotate
on the screen.
In shame we come

together.

YOU HAVE JUST DINED...

"You have just dined, and however scrupulously the slaughterhouse is concealed in the graceful distance of miles, there is complicity."

—Ralph Waldo Emerson

Are animals our fellow beings on this planet?
If they are, does that mean that we should eat them?
Does it mean that we should not eat them?
Does it mean that it doesn't matter whether we eat them or not?

To some, it seems very clear that animals are our fellow beings, and that we should not eat them.
To others, it is equally clear that they are not in any real sense our fellow beings, and that we should eat them.
Others say that animals are our fellow beings, but that we should eat them anyway if we want to.
Most seem to believe that we should eat some of them, whether or not they are our fellow beings, but not others, who, presumably, are.

I find all this very confusing.

KISS ME

How many times am I going to have to
tell you about Michael Smith?
That extraterrestrial in this strange
land who knew
in his bones
how to kiss?
And all he did was pay
attention
to it.
Exquisite attention, granted.
But they fainted—
those women he kissed—
most of them.

They fainted. And all
Michael Smith did
was pay exquisite attention to
what was going on during
each moment as it passed.
He never thought of
what would happen next.

And they fainted.

Why do you think I keep telling you
about Michael Smith?

ZOOMINOOSHA

Sitting in a cage of snakes
for fifty days to break
the world snake-sitting
record, I realized,
during an odd moment of concentration,
that I no longer loved you.

You weren't among the watchers, press,
who wished me well, no doubt,
as I sat, unmoving…unnaturally
still, one might say,
disregarding the circumstances.

Which was just as well.
Glass would have been
the thinnest thing
between us.

I'd refused your kiss, remember?

For though I know that snakes
do not, like bees, dart for honey,
do not, buzzardlike, smell despair,
still I feared some psychochemical
residue,
decided kissing was a
bad idea.

Instead, we discussed anomalies.
Like ligers, which
can
happen, when a male lion
and a tigress
are given no alternatives.

Snake caging rules are few
and sane:
be still. Or be slow,
refuse them no path, don't twitch
when they spit behind you.
(The cameras will catch all that,
you can watch with a lover, later.)

Which reminds me:
It was only after taking
and developing
a hundred stills of small cracks
in concrete pavements
—on the hundred and first—
that I loved you to begin with.
And you weren't there
then, either.

CAN BREAK-OUT BE STOPPED?
(Pamphlet #1, Clinique Information Series)

Yes, says Clinique, frankly.
Either stopped cold
or controlled
in the vast majority of cases.
But I think not.
After all,
good surface care
lacks depth
by definition, and
can't really deal with those tiny
depressions, regressions, ensuing regrets.
Clinique forgets
sooner or later.
A definite relationship between the menses and
break-out has been established.
Clever of Clinique to notice this.
What I've noticed are menses tendencies
to consider breaking out but then
wind up breaking down - to
deny, even, the occasional clarity
just because it
must be chemical.

So what if the burgeoning blood says, "Leave.
Get out now; the work is wrong," or, "The man's
no mate." (Blood's frequently wise; coagulates
quickly in wounds sustained while believing it.)

Is it correct to say that troubled skin is a thing of the past?
Clinique thinks so. Says
Most people have no idea how unnecessary it is to suffer
through a period or a lifetime of unhappy skin.
Ah, well...
Periods yes. Lifetimes no.
There's always
sooner or later.

MENSTRUAL MYTHOLOGY

Hey, loony woman,
does your moon coincide with this hemisphere's moon?
Is that why you say what you say?

Your tune's a rag flute serenade
to a moon dipped in blood from the harpy lamb
whose throat is slit by the sickle moon
who kills the ram,
rapes the wheat and reaps the weight of golden hair
of weeping earth, the mother ewe, watching.

Hey, loony woman,
do your moons collide to a hemos fear's tune?
Are you twice on the rag today?

THE BONES OF THE LAMBS

The bones of the lambs
that had been dead for days…

the bones that were their ribs
that I have torn through broiled flesh
to get to with my teeth…

these ribs, that then have soaked for days
and dried for weeks…

how many and how difficult
the scrapings
the sandings
to clean them,
shape them into smooth suggestions
suspicions,

how fiercely and too late
the ligaments cling to bone,
and
to their mandate to
connect
rib and lower rib
rib and tip of
cleavered spine

as though life required
only
extreme
resistance.

A WORD SOMETIMES

A word sometimes can rule a day
in much the way a god or nature
can be understood to rule
and then be felt there
waiting
to be worshipped
for existing.
Today's word
is schadenfreude.

Photographable Vulnerability

WHEN I WAS A CHILD

When I was a child
barefoot in New Orleans
at the corner of Bourbon and St. Philip
I used to watch the tourists.
I used to stare at them, in fact,
and they stared back at me.

(Later I "became," as they say,
an actress.)

FOR JIM WAY, DIRECTOR

(What was it you used to call yourself? A "secondary artist?")

There should be something more than misery now.
What went between us for so long was never
one thing; always
more than this simple
sweet
shriek
of liquid sadness, clinging like ocean
to the spinning rock of ache that
seems to locate close to where
I know my heart stays
and beats,
still,
spinning…
though it slows oddly when I try to find it
sense the spinning…
I think of it
and it stills, instantly.

Ah, fear is here.
Welcome.
Before I can forbid myself to
wonder whether oceans slip
when hearts stop
spinning,
sadness has company;
quiets.

Stay, fear.
I wish to contemplate internal drowning,
picture my lungs as dead fish, my spleen
the flotsam of complex industrial waste,
my heart some sole survivor on a bony island
shouting
to be left alone.
No, stay, fear.

You give my mind much more the look of life.

I knew, while we loved,
that I always would.
What consolation is this, that
that small thing was true?
Why, while we hated, did I never say,
"Bastard! You bastard, I'll bury you"?
That too would have been true.

PHOTOGRAPHABLE VULNERABILITY

1.
The people I live with tread softly
but are annoyed this morning.
What offends them?

All this energy
while I'm gearing up to work,
this closing down and opening out,
this brewing of storm before calm?

This willful and frenzied
assembling and taking
of prerogatives?

This agreement with myself
to be ready…is it so difficult to make
that nothing else
can seem agreeable
to me?

2.
Actors
meeting before work
in some location restaurant
show each other courtesies,
give benefits of doubts.
With one another they seem
fairly relaxed.

I know, though,
if I were this one's mate
—that one's mother—
we would not have fared so well together
over breakfast.

3.
What they want is the top of you. Skin.
The look and the
way and the lay of the land of you, in
little
boxes.
How the boxes jive,
how they sizzle together, and
how electric is it?
The surface voltage of this apparition?
What you've acquired is very important.
Experience and the lines of this.
or lack of them.
An air, a walk, a style of speaking, friends in the business, clarities,
scars.
PHO-TO-GRAPHABLE VUL-NERA-BILITY

4.
Ah, Jan, I love you with all the shame and joy of unwilling
reawakening…as only an actress who has loved a father (who
died) and then a director (who died on her father's birthday)
can love another director. How hopeful it is that you live-
how fearful this hope, for I loved them too well not to fear
their deaths, but still they died. This is indeed a most joy-
ful, shameful, hopeful, unwilling love—a fearful love of your
life. My being sang so with it tonight, and with the love I
felt you feeling for me as you worked and waited for my love
and my tears,
I could not even cry for you—until later, from another shame,
over not having been able to do it…

PHOTO-GRAPHABLE VULNERA-BILITY

5.
"You vill tell me ven you are ready, yes?
Ve vill vait.
Ven you are ready, ve begin."
She tries to see inside her eyes, probes her throat for a lump,
digs around for memories of the two deaths in her life, that

shouldn't have healed, but did. Now she knows. They shouldn't
have healed.
And she is not sentimental.
He is waiting, patient, like a lizard, lidded eyes and lips
drawn back, unblinking, leaning toward her across the corpse,
tabled, sheeted; an actor trying not to breathe or fall asleep.
My son, she thinks. My son is dead, and her hand moves to touch
him. Mistake. He quivers; she has touched too near the groin,
surprised him. Close to her she hears nose breath released in a
smile. Feet shift on the floor behind her. The extras are
restless. The crew is bored and tired. But this will go on until she can find
the tears.
Earlier in the evening she had stepped to the rail of the second story
porch outside this room.
She had looked out over the land, felt air on her cheeks, and
in the energy of true concentration had summoned the tears,
Exhilarated, she had thought, yes, it's all there, ready, and
carefully calmed herself, saving, storing. But now it was gone.
There was no tension in the air now. Only boredom.
Adrenaline was spent hours ago. How did one do it now, without
juice, without the rush, without certainty, determination,
confidence?

PHOTOGRAPHABLEVULNER-ABILITY.

6.

And it doesn't help, Jan, that you move like Jim—my other
director. And probably for the same reason—your back.
You know, I suppose, that people who feel great and complex
responsibility and have never learned, viscerally, to delegate
it often have "back trouble." When weight is put upon a person,
then he can resist what he does not want, and the conflict will
be in his gut. But the nature of your work is the choice of
that weight, as well as the weight of the choice. Minds mold
bodies and muscles and organs, and you are stuck with the standard
of a prehistoric rightness from which you fall dangerously short.
So your body rebels and you compensate as best you can, carrying
yourself still further into mind, blinding yourself still further
to your body's begging for an equal chance...

140

PHOTO —

You smoke cigarettes constantly, with joy and self hatred…

GRAPHABLE

The tiny exuberant puff, the immediate exhalation of some of
the smoke, and then the deliberate and habituated inhalation
of what's left…

VULNERABILITY…

You are born and die a thousand times an hour.

PHOTOGRAPHABLEVULNERABILITY.

7.
As in other jobs, you must show up on time,
come prepared to work,
remember words,
forget slights, indignities, promises.

What you're producing is product.
Remember.
They do. Or they die.
Unless you can make them
forget, for an instant,
as you somehow take heart,
find art
while cranking out product.

THE HUNGARIAN HAIR STYLIST

The Hungarian hair stylist combs me out, fills me in
on his life, about which he plans to write a book. It
seems that no one told him who he was, till he was twenty.
Then, from her die-bed, his grandmother wrote him.
It was time. He must know,
he was not who he was, but someone else.
He'd been born the son of trashy next-door neighbors,

This small seed of fact became a mighty oak in seconds,
acorns dropping over acres of his mind.
Soon he was lost in that forest.
All was twisted, knarled and old,
he was stunned and cold and crying;
he told a tree he'd sinned and now must die,
for now he knew he'd been fucking his sister.

Weeks later, still trying to die (by crying and not
fucking his sister,) he was visited by his grandmother
in her shroud. She took his hand, led him away, showed
him a new land, from the clouds. Years later, this turned out
to be the view from a DC 10 of Los Angeles,
where he was going to do his first American film. He had
a hundred and fifty actors to make up every day, with no help

but one poosey face doing touch-up on the set, which was
in the middle of a desert. He couldn't speak the language yet,
which deaded his personality and caused all the actors to
hate him in his guts. This made him decide to suicide himself
again (by crying and fucking to death poosey-face in his tent.)
Now once more in a dream came the grandmother. She took his
hand, led him away through years, showed him a palatial room.

All ferns and tiles, carpets, no counters or notting like dat,
just beautiful furnitures around a little, you know, like dat,
and it vas called De Temple for Beauty, very niiice. All this
would be his in time, she promised, and please to be more calmer,
please to act more better, please to get his ass in gear and
scrape himself together. And this would come to pass, he knew, and
found his ears were ringing with the click of curling irons and the

songs of angels singing. Someday. He will have his Temple for Beauty,
and I will go to it. If I can afford it. I will even buy his book,
which he will write in Hungarian and then have translated by someone
sensitive. (For now, he pulls my hair, and I tell him where his English
is wrong. "But vat ees dis 'of?' he argues.) Still, I hope the Temple
doesn't come too soon. He's wonderful with hair. And then, on the set,
he stays right with you. You don't have to see a mirror all day long.

IN AND OUT OF THE DREAM

In this dream
I've been dreaming of you.
Rich, satisfying dreams,
seemingly devoid of symbolism.

We are talking, sitting close together at a table.
Near you, resting on the table,
lies my arm—
the part of it that begins at the elbow,
ends at the wrist—and then my hand is there.
Everything is normal.

My arm is attached to me in the normal fashion.
At the shoulder.

Magically, though, there is no cigarette.
I am not smoking; nor are you.
This, I see now, is odd.

You place your hand upon my arm, then
Your face down next to your hand,
partly resting on it, all the warm weight
of your hand and your head, on my arm.
You don't look up at me.

In these dreams, the intimacy of this
has been too much dreamed of.
For a moment, I can't breathe.

I put my face down next to yours, barely touching.
We breathe each other's air.
We barely smile.
I don't know whether you are comforting me
or asking to be comforted.

For in this dream I know
you feel the weight of all
the dreams of you being dreamed,
and now, as I dream too,
you come to me. Why?
To share the burden?
To gloat?
No one dreams of me. I'm free.
Were it not for you,
I'd float.

MOVABLE WALLS

We are actresses
playing whores.
We joke with the crew as they
stare at us
through the real windows
of a room with movable walls.
With thumbs and forefingers
we make that gesture that means
"money"; motion to them to come round to the doors.
they laugh at us
so we play some more at
being whores for them
and it does seem funny.
But we feel fleeting
things behind their eyes
and ours
and we think
that they really do laugh
at us but don't know why.
Do they wonder
what it means for us
to laugh at playing whores
wonder whether whores would laugh
wonder if we know?

PAST DEATHS

Your life, they say
will flash before you as you die.

Your deaths, though, are what you think of
as you lie there on the floor,
once more
being killed for camera.

That time, ten hours in a coffin, wearing a dress so old,
close fitting, fragile,
that one deep breath could rip the fabric.
Leaving the coffin required a man at either elbow
lifting you,
fully braced,
zombie-like
from supine to standing.

And that day you decided people surely didn't
fall so neatly to the floor when killed;
what was wrong with all those actors?
And so you toppled "realistically,"
a rag doll thrown down anyhow.
Before noon, you did this.
By dark
you had found time for regrets,
sorrows for your judgments.

Today
I lie down on the killing floor
unconcerned
with choices.
My position will be negotiated
between director and cameraman
in some other language.
I am free to think
whatever will please me now
or surely later
when I think back
on it.

My eyes are closed
or almost.
Languages flow past me
like all my deaths
and eventually it transpires that
there is to be a slight curving of my
carefully
comfortably
arranged
body.

Mimicking the arc of the round table above me? Nice.
A turn of my neck toward that table.

Ah. Closer to the table. Up against the chair leg.
This will have the virtue of realistic awkwardness
which will be offset by eventual pain
from pressing too long against the chair leg but
never mind.
I am my favorite thing to be;
an instrument
of someone's vision.
At times my own
today another's.

(And then
when Willem enters,
he'll have more room to maneuver
between me and the wall.)

Now the blood arrives on set
in plastic squeeze bottles.
Syrup bottles, ketchup bottles;
mayonnaise and mustard bottles.
Werner decides where sword thrusts had entered,
where blood would pool,
where fall into artistic curlicues above my head.
He, only he, is the squeezer.
More blood is brought in, more is called for.
This blood is too light!
Darker blood!
More darker blood!
Now some lighter!

More lighter!
The spent plastic bottles are quickly collected,
returned
to the mixers of blood,
who by now are frantic.
More blood!
More blood!
Now he dumps it from a large glass pickle jar
as that is what's been handed him.

She chooses not to feel humiliated
when a plastic honey bear squirts blood
onto her cheekbone,
slightly up her nose,
but all goes quiet as the dead might be.
This death seems new at last, and
she is not remembering much
until a backfire on the street reminds her of the hours
she spent years ago as pigeons standing in for bats were
unsuccessfully encouraged to fly up en masse—
but much more quickly, please—Jesus!
from her shotgunned body.
Even the handy shot gun could not produce a scare for pigeons.

Bright yellow plastic sheeting is thrown over her.
She knows she must be very
still,
so as not to
smear the blood, not
flinch,
as Willem is to come in,
bend over,
and sweep the yellow sheet from all of her at once.

What menace is he meant to infuriate with this
bullfighter's gesture?

We are not used to these grand exposures, but have
learned the way it's done, haven't we?
One corner lifted, all the coroners and their
churlish unveilings…
I.D. the goal, not revelation
tamping down the shock, not
ramping it up—impossible—too easy!

But just because it's easy doesn't mean it's not worthwhile.

All she really wants to know is if,
somehow,
in the edited scene,
the gesture will be darkly
funny.

And if blood drying now
in the crevice between right buttock
and thigh
is as thick as it feels, and if she'll be able to
wash it all off
before lunch is half over.

NOTE TO A PRODUCER

Never fear tainting the pathos.
If we are forced to laugh when we
want to cry,
what more can sadness show us?

THE HOLE

The hole has been dug
through the sound stage floor.
Neat edges.
Wide for a grave; a bit shallow.
Four feet deep into the earth beneath.

Scenes are shot in front of it,
like me poring lime down into it.
Like me feeding my tied-up husband
his last meal of Kentucky Fried Chicken and biscuits.

Then crew fills the hole back up, unevenly, so
I can get down into it, and seem to be
early
in the process of digging
this hole in my
little shed.

I am proud of this hole
I have not dug myself
(and proud of not falling into it
when I have to run past it.)
I am aware of my pride in this hole
I am pretending to dig—
aware of my pride in its perfectly vertical walls—
amused by my pride and not
embarrassed by it.

Pride is only one of
many things I feel and don't feel,
remember and forget,
shove into
deep background
and don't think about.

That is what we are,
aren't we—
all the things we're not thinking about ?

All I have to do is
just
keep digging.

photo by Nelly Recchia | www.nellyrecchia.com

Grace Zabriskie has been writing poems for over thirty years. She is also a visual artist and an actor, currently a regular on the HBO series *Big Love*.

www.gracezabriskie.com

About NYQ Books™

NYQ Books™ was established in 2009 as an imprint of The New York Quarterly Foundation, Inc. Its mission is to augment the New York Quarterly poetry magazine by providing an additional venue for poets already published in the magazine. A lifelong dream of NYQ's founding editor, William Packard, NYQ Books™ has been made possible by both growing foundation support and new technology that was not available during William Packard's lifetime. We are proud to present these books to you and hope that you will continue to support The New York Quarterly Foundation, Inc. and our poets and that you will enjoy these other titles from NYQ Books™:

Joanna Crispi	*Soldier in the Grass*
Ted Jonathan	*Bones and Jokes*
Amanda J. Bradley	*Hints and Allegations*
Fred Yannantuono	*A Boilermaker for the Lady*
Ira Joe Fisher	*Songs from an Earlier Century*
Kevin Pilkington	*In the Eyes of a Dog*
Tony Quagliano	*Language Matters*

Please visit our website for these and other titles:

www.nyqbooks.org